Vietnam

Karen O'Connor

🌿 Carolrhoda Books, Inc. / Minneapolis

Photo Acknowledgments

Photos, maps, and artworks are used courtesy of John Erste, pp. 1, 2–3, 7, 16–17, 21, 31, 33, 38–39; Laura Westlund, pp. 4, 24–25, 43; © TRIP/J. Sweeney, pp. 6 (left), 16, 35 (top); Rick and Susie Graetz, pp. 6 (right), 7, 14, 18 (both), 22, 22–23, 26 (bottom), 28, 30; © Nevada Wier, pp. 8, 10 (bottom), 11 (bottom), 12 (top), 15 (both), 17 (left), 25 (both), 29, 31, 32 (both), 33, 36, 37 (both), 40, 44; © TRIP/N. Kealey, p. 9 (left); © TRIP/R. Squires, p. 9 (right); © TRIP/H. Bower, pp. 10 (top), 35 (bottom); © John Elk III, pp. 11 (top), 13, 17 (right), 19, 27, 41 (bottom), 43; © TRIP/A. Tovy, p. 12 (bottom); © Brian A. Vikander, p. 20 (left); © TRIP/A. Ghazzal, pp. 20 (right), 26 (top); © Sophie Dauwe/Robert Fried Photography, pp. 23, 41 (top); © TRIP/R. Nichols, p. 24; © TRIP/B.Vikander, pp. 34, 42; Cover photo of Vietnamese boat by © Rick Graetz.

Carolrhoda Books, Inc.
A Division of the Lerner Publishing Group
241 First Avenue North
Minneapolis, Minnesota 55401 U.S.A.

Website address: www.lernerbooks.com

Words in **bold type** are explained in a glossary that begins on page 44.

Library of Congress Cataloging-in-Publication Data

O'Connor, Karen, 1938–
    Vietnam / by Karen O'Connor.
      p. cm. — (Globe-trotters club)
    Includes index.
    Summary: Examines the history, geography, folklore, society, economy, and culture of Vietnam.
    ISBN 1–57505–117–6 (lib. bdg. : alk. paper)
    1. Vietnam—Juvenile Literature. [1. Vietnam.] I. Title. II. Series: Globe-trotters club (Series).
DS556.3.016 1999
959.7—dc21   98–46344

Manufactured in the United States of America
1 2 3 4 5 6 – JR – 04 03 02 01 00 99

Contents

CHINA

Mount
Fan Si Pan ▲ — Red River

V I E T N A M

Hanoi ★

Haiphong

SOUTH
CHINA
SEA

Gulf
of
Tonkin

CHINA

L
A
O
S

N

Mekong River

A
N
N
A
M
I
T
E

M
O
U
N
T
A
I
N
S

Hue
Da
Nang

Chao Mung den Vietnam!*

*That's "Welcome to Vietnam" in Vietnamese, the language of Vietnam.

I n d o c h i n a

P e n i n s u l a

C A M B O D I A

Mekong River

Ho Chi Minh
City

Miles

0   50   100   150

0   100   200

Kilometers

SOUTH
CHINA
SEA

〰 mountains
⁄⁄⁄ highlands
≈ lowlands
▨ deltas
★ capital city

Long, thin Vietnam hugs the South China Sea, which links to the vast Pacific Ocean. Vietnam is in **Indochina,** a **peninsula** that separates the South China Sea from the Bay of Bengal, part of the Indian Ocean.

High, forested mountains called the Annamite Range spread over the western edge of the country. The peaks separate Vietnam from its neighbors Laos and Cambodia. Mountains and high **plains** stretch into China, Vietnam's neighbor to the north. And guess what? The central highlands in the middle of Vietnam are hilly and high, too. But the land slopes downward near the coast.

River **deltas** dominate the low-lying parts of Vietnam. In the south, the Mekong River breaks into hundreds of smaller rivers that empty into the South China Sea. The Red River Delta, in northeastern Vietnam, meets the Gulf of Tonkin (part of the South China Sea). Wet, green fields called rice paddies blanket the river deltas. Most Vietnamese people live in villages and towns along the deltas.

Fast Facts about Vietnam

Name: Socialist Republic of Vietnam
Area: 130,468 square miles
Main Landforms: Mekong River Delta, Red River Delta, Annamite Mountain Range, coastal lowlands, northern highlands
Highest Point: Mount Fan Si Pan (10,306 feet)
Lowest Point: Sea level
Major Rivers: Mekong River, Red River
Animals: Asian elephant, python, water buffalo
Capital City: Hanoi
Other Major Cities: Ho Chi Minh City, Haiphong, Hue, Da Nang
Official Language: Vietnamese
Money Unit: Dong

Wind and *Water*

Vietnam has perfect rice-growing conditions. Rice seedlings thrive in the marshy, water-soaked soil.

Vietnam has a **tropical** climate. The weather never feels cold. In the northern mountains, winter weather can be cool—about 65 degrees—but it warms up to the 80s in the spring. The hot and steamy lowlands are in the 80s or higher year-round.

Rain hardly ever stops in Vietnam. It drizzles almost every spring day. In the winter, **monsoons** batter northern Vietnam with rain. Summer monsoons bring heavy rainstorms to southern and central Vietnam.

Watch out for floods! All that rain can make the Red River rise 30 feet in a single day—that's as high as a three-story building. Typhoons can cause even more damage to coastal towns. These violent storms speed from the Indian and Pacific Oceans to strike Vietnam's coast with huge waves and powerful winds.

All that rain might not sound like fun, but the Vietnamese are used to it. And plants love Vietnam's hot, rainy climate. Farmers grow thin rubber trees near Ho Chi Minh City. Fruits like bananas, guavas, and

The Vietnamese must be prepared for rain at any time on every day of the year.

The Monsoon Story

My Nuong, a princess, wanted to marry. Both Spirit of the Sea and Spirit of the Mountain wanted to be her husband. The two men set out to bring her gifts, and the princess decided to marry the first one to arrive. When Spirit of the Mountain arrived first, the princess married him. Spirit of the Sea arrived soon after and was furious to have missed his chance. He told his soldiers to steal the princess away from Spirit of the Mountain. Wind blew, rain fell, and the ocean rose to flood the shore.

The bride and groom dashed up the mountain. Their army threw tree trunks and boulders down toward the soldiers of the sea, who were coming quickly after them. Spirit of the Mountain cast a spell to make his mountain home go higher. Spirit of the Sea could no longer reach the bride and groom. But every summer, he tries to win the princess by sending storms and floods—a monsoon—to the foot of the mountain.

jackfruit (a sweet-tasting, yellow fruit) thrive. Farmers can raise two or even three crops of rice every year. That means lots of food for the Vietnamese!

The Red River, named for the color of its muddy water, can flood its banks during times of heavy rain.

Bamboo for sale! People make furniture, tools, cooking utensils, and more from bamboo, which can grow 120 feet tall.

Green **Forests**

Vietnam's forests stay green all year-round. In the north, bamboo (a woody grass) and hardwood trees cover the mountains and highlands. Tropical evergreens and palm trees fill **rain forests** in the southwestern mountains and in the lowlands. **Mangrove** trees hedge the coasts and the wet deltas.

Poisonous snakes, tiny monkeys, and wild pigs live in forests. In the rain forests, herds of Asian elephants roam. On hot days, they use their trunks to toss reddish soil onto their gray hides. The dirt cools the elephants. But it also makes their skin look red!

Some people cut trees down to create farmland. They use elephants

8

to drag the logs away from the fields! The wood is made into sturdy, valuable furniture or used to build houses or boats. More farmland means that farmers can grow more food. But some rain-forest animals have nowhere to go. In the 1980s, Vietnamese people began replanting efforts to save forested areas.

Thick vegetation crowds the Mekong River Delta (left). **Farmers cut fields into the sides of steep mountains** (above). **Vietnam is losing much of its valuable rain forest to farmland.**

Who lives **in Vietnam?**

 More than 78 million people live in Vietnam. And about 40 percent of them are younger than 15 years old. That's a lot of kids!

The **ethnic Vietnamese,** who have black hair and brown eyes, make up about 85 percent of Vietnam's population. Their **ancestors** include long-ago Chinese settlers who made their homes in the Red River Delta. The settlers married members of other **ethnic groups** who moved to the area from islands in the Pacific Ocean. Over time their descendents became the ethnic Vietnamese.

Other ethnic groups live in Vietnam, too. Many Chinese traders settled in Vietnam about 200 years ago. Their modern-day relatives

This Chinese-Vietnamese man (left top) **shares long-ago ancestors with these ethnic Vietnamese kids** (left bottom).

Ancient towers remind visitors of the Champa kingdom that stood near the Mekong Delta. Descendants of the original Cham still live in the area.

speak Chinese and Vietnamese. Most live in Vietnam's big cities of Hanoi and Ho Chi Minh City. The Cham live in central Vietnam, where they once ruled a kingdom called Champa. Many Khmer people farm in southern Vietnam. The Tay choose mountain homes.

Montagnards

In French the word *montagnard* means "highlander." Some of Vietnam's ethnic groups—such as the Hmong, Red Zao, and Tai—like life in the mountains. Together, these people are known as the Montagnards. Most Montagnards speak both Vietnamese and their own languages. Many Montagnards are nomads, hunters, or farmers.

Members of the Red Zao minority

Family *Life*

Vietnamese people like big families. In years past, couples often had 10 or 12 children! These days the government asks that parents have only two children to keep the population from growing too much, but families of four or five kids remain standard. Even if parents don't have a lot of children, extended families—which include grandparents, cousins, aunts, and uncles—like to live

A young Vietnamese girl gives her mom a hand (above). More than 78 million people live in Vietnam. A newlywed couple poses for pictures with members of their families (below).

together. With all those people, everyone tries to cooperate and get along.

Kids are supposed to respect and obey their parents and other adults. Older people are considered wise and experienced. Youngsters might help their parents by shopping, cooking, cleaning, and caring for the youngest and oldest family members.

Most Vietnamese adults get married. In the past, parents picked whom their children would marry. These days most people choose

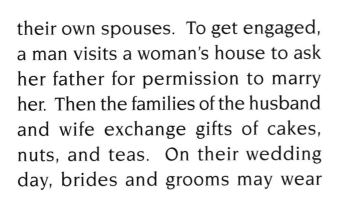

All in the Family

Try these Vietnamese words out on your family!
Can they understand you?

grandfather	*ong*	(OONG)
grandmother	*ba*	(BAH)
father	*cha*	(CHAH)
mother	*ma*	(MAH)
uncle	*bac*	(BAHK)
aunt	*co*	(COH)
son	*con tai*	(cahn TYE)
daughter	*con gai*	(cahn GYE)
older brother	*ahn*	(AHN)
younger brother	*trai*	(TRY)
older sister	*chi*	(CHIH)
younger sister	*gai*	(GY)

their own spouses. To get engaged, a man visits a woman's house to ask her father for permission to marry her. Then the families of the husband and wife exchange gifts of cakes, nuts, and teas. On their wedding day, brides and grooms may wear traditional Vietnamese clothes. As part of the ceremony, each eats a piece of ginger root dipped in salt. The harsh taste reminds them of challenges they might face together. Then everyone goes to the groom's house for a huge feast!

It seems that every type of fruit or vegetable you could imagine is sold on city streets.

The Big **Cities**

Ho Chi Minh City in the south is the biggest city. In the north is Hanoi, Vietnam's capital. About one in every five Vietnamese people lives in a city.

In the daytime, city streets fill with people walking everywhere. Walkers watch out for the motorbikes, bicycles, and *cyclos* (tricycles that carry passengers). Beep, beep!

14

At street markets, people bargain, hoping to get a good deal. Vendors sell delicious treats like fried bananas or meatballs. Handmade crafts are a popular buy. Farmers and gardeners sell fresh fruits and vegetables. At sidewalk cafes, friends chat and play card games.

Every day people leave the countryside to settle in Vietnam's cities. To make homes for all the newcomers, lots of folks construct new apartment buildings. Other city dwellers choose jobs in government offices, as medical workers, and as teachers. Some people labor in factories or run their own businesses.

Yikes! Better watch your step in this city traffic jam (left). **A family of four hitches a ride on a cyclo** (above).

15

At Home **on the Farm**

About 80 percent of Vietnamese people live in small villages surrounded by flat, watery rice paddies! At planting time, the fields look like ponds. But soon the paddies are green with growing rice plants.

Vegetable gardens and fruit trees surround houses. Lots of farmers raise soybeans or cotton as well as

Water buffalo pull plows and carts in rural Vietnam. When their work is done, they like to cool off in canals, rivers, and streams.

rice. When kids aren't at school, they have chores. Girls help with sewing, cooking, and washing clothes. Boys carry water, help with the farming or fishing, and feed the animals. And everyone helps harvest rice! Farmers give some of their crops to the government, which uses it to make sure people in cities have enough to eat. Farmers keep or sell the rest at open-air markets.

These kids are hard at work helping with their family's rice harvest.

Cruising Canals

Canals link rivers and streams to fields. Farmers use the canals to water their rice paddies. But that's not all they're for! People paddle bamboo canoes to visit neighbors or to go fishing. Other people stock their boats with rice, fish, coconuts, chickens, and vegetables to sell at floating markets. They don't have to unload. At floating markets, the goods stay on the boats!

Using his chopsticks expertly, a customer at a city street cafe nabs a tasty seasoning for his bowl of rice (above). **A woman uses age-old techniques to separate rice grains from the stalks** (right).

What's **Cooking?**

You guessed it—rice! If you sit down for breakfast in a Vietnamese household you won't find cereal on the table. You'll eat rice, a bowl of noodle soup called *pho,* and fruit.

Vietnamese people eat rice at just about every meal. Cooks add rice and rice noodles to soups, and they serve it with tasty sauces. N*uoc cham*—a yummy blend of vinegar or lime juice, sugar, chopped garlic,

Drink Up!

On a hot day, Vietnamese kids love to sip soda *chanh*. You can make one, too!

You will need:
- A drinking glass
- A spoon
- I lemon
- 2 cups of soda water
- I teaspoon sugar
- I cup of crushed ice*

Cut the lemon in half and squeeze the juice from both halves. Next, fill the drinking glass with crushed ice. Add the lemon juice. Fill the rest of the glass with soda water. Carefully stir in a teaspoon of sugar. Enjoy that tasty soda chanh!

*Crushed ice is for sale at most grocery and convenience stores. Or you can fill a heavy-duty plastic bag with ice cubes and, with an adult, smash the cubes into small bits with a hammer or a rolling pin.

A rice-noodle vendor awaits her next customer at an outdoor market.

and minced chili pepper—is added to fish, meat, and vegetables.

At dinnertime people sit on the floor around a low table loaded with a pot of rice and steaming bowls of vegetables, fish, pork, beef, or bean curd (also known as tofu). They use chopsticks—thin, wooden sticks—to pick up tasty morsels. And some folks wash it down with rice wine! When they eat noodle soup, Vietnamese people use chopsticks to eat the rice noodles. Then they slurp the broth straight from the bowl. In Vietnam, that's considered polite!

The Army Museum in Hanoi records the country's long history of war.

Historically
Speaking . . .

China ruled most of modern-day Vietnam until a Vietnamese emperor took charge in A.D. 939. Nearly 600 years later, French and Portuguese traders had arrived in Vietnam. By 1883 France had control of **French Indochina.** The French built railroads, government buildings, and

So Long, Saigon!

Ho Chi Minh City used to be called Saigon. When the northern and southern parts of Vietnam reunited, Saigon was renamed in honor of Ho Chi Minh, an important Vietnamese leader. When Ho Chi Minh died in 1969, a huge building was constructed in Hanoi to be his grave. Lots of Vietnamese people visit the structure to remember Ho Chi Minh.

large plantations (farms). But the Vietnamese people were harshly treated and heavily taxed.

War broke out in 1945, after the Vietnamese declared independence from France. Vietnam won in 1954. When the Vietnamese couldn't agree on what kind of government to have, the northern and southern parts of the country split apart.

Each side wanted to rule the other, and the two were soon at war. The fighting lasted for many years. Peace was declared in 1973, and two years later, the nation united under a type of government called **Communism.** War continued until 1989, as Vietnam fought with its neighboring countries.

The war years were sad and hard. Families were separated when men left to fight. Cities, towns, villages, and fields were bombed. Many thousands of people died. These days Vietnamese people try to put the wars behind them by working to make Vietnam a good place to live.

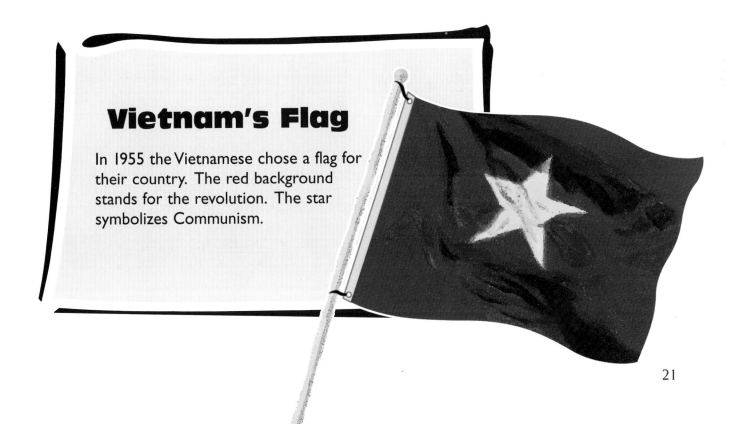

Vietnam's Flag

In 1955 the Vietnamese chose a flag for their country. The red background stands for the revolution. The star symbolizes Communism.

Don't get up on the wrong side of the bed in one of these houses. You might end up in the river. Splash!

Going **Home**

At the end of the school day, Vietnamese kids head to all kinds of houses. Most city dwellers live in apartment buildings. Big families squeeze into a few tiny rooms.

In the northern countryside, people build small houses of stone or wood. In the warm, humid south, families choose larger houses made of wood and bamboo. Tightly woven straw roofs keep out the heavy rain.

Near rivers and canals, some houses perch on stilts. The tall poles keep homes safe from floods in the wet season. In the dry season, women weave cloth in the cool shade under their houses.

22

Houses and apartment buildings are only part of Vietnam's architecture. Ancient palaces crumble in the countryside. Some structures show Chinese influence. Statues and scenes from Chinese literature decorate temples. And in cities such as Hanoi, it's easy to spot structures with a French accent! These buildings are usually painted yellow and have detailed ironwork, shuttered windows, and wide front steps.

A Chinese structure

In the mountains, as many as 40 family members might live in one narrow longhouse! Workers construct longhouses from palm branches, sugarcane leaves, and wooden planks.

Many dwellings, such as this longhouse, don't have electricity or running water. People get water from pumps or from rivers. After dark lanterns light the way.

23

A fierce dragon breathes fire in this detail of a lacquerware item.

Handmade Art

Vietnam has a long tradition of handmade goods. Many beautiful crafts are for sale at open-air markets in Vietnam's towns and cities. A district of Hanoi, called 36 Streets, is the place to find 36 different crafts—one on each street!

Ceramics (pottery) is a popular art form in Vietnam. A family of artisans may have a shop. Parents and children mold clay into pots, cups, vases, and plates. The pottery is baked in a kiln (hot oven) until it is hard and white. Then artisans glaze the pieces with delicate blue-and-white designs.

Lacquerware is another popular art form. Artists shape pieces of wood into boxes, vases, and furniture. They decorate the wood and apply seven coats of a clear, glossy liquid called lacquer. Each layer of lacquer takes seven days to dry.

Block printing, a method of making patterned cloth and paper, is popular, too. Workers carve patterns, flowers, or scenes from daily life onto flat blocks of wood. Then, they ink the block before pressing it onto paper or cloth. The ink leaves a beautiful design.

A family displays examples of woodblock artwork.

Silk's Story

Making silk is a traditional Vietnamese craft. Workers unravel **silkworm** cocoons and weave the strands into silk, a rich fabric that is used for fancy clothes. Vietnamese people don't just weave cloth. Using bamboo they weave round boats that look like big baskets. Artisans weave hats, mats, and baskets from straw, rice stalks, and grass.

Get **Dressed!**

People in Vietnam wear all sorts of clothes. City dwellers might choose stylish suits or dresses. But across Vietnam, most men and women dress in cotton shirts and pants. Workers roll up the legs of their pants to keep the fabric dry in the wet fields and rice paddies. A *non la* (a cone-shaped, woven hat) is great for keeping off the hot sun or the pouring rain.

Cool and comfortable are rules of dress in the countryside (left). **City clothes in Vietnam are more fancy** (above). **The driver wears a bandanna for wind protection.**

On special occasions, men and women like to wear traditional Vietnamese clothing. A man might choose a loose tunic (a knee-length, loose-fitting shirt) over pants. Over long pants, women put on *ao dai*, which is a long, fitted tunic slit up to the waist. Young Vietnamese women especially like to wear ao dai. They may also wear high-heeled wooden sandals. Kids usually choose shirts and pants, like their parents do, and go barefoot.

School **Daze**

Study hard! In Vietnam education is highly respected. So kids try to do their best in school. Most schools don't have many books or teachers. To keep class sizes down, one group of students attends school from early morning until midday. A second group takes classes in the afternoon.

Vietnamese children aged 6 to 11 attend primary school. They learn reading, writing, and math skills. Some youngsters attend secondary school (high school), but most kids leave school to work.

No one ever gets a bad grade in Vietnam! Instead of report cards, teachers send a note home to each

In some schools, children wear a uniform of white shirts and red ties. But at this school, anything goes. How would you like to go to class barefoot once in a while?

Nine out of ten Vietnamese can read and write.

In addition to learning reading, math, science, and social studies, Vietnamese students are taught traditional manners and customs.

student's parents. The notes tell how the kid is doing in school. And there's no such thing as summer vacation! All year long, students attend class six days a week. But in the countryside, students take time off from school to help their parents harvest crops.

Statues of Buddha in a typical pose and wearing a peaceful expression remind Buddhists to separate themselves from worldly possessions.

A Mix of **Faiths**

The government of Vietnam doesn't encourage religions in the country, but more than half of the Vietnamese people practice Buddhism. Followers of Buddhism believe in a cycle of life and rebirth, in peace, and in cooperation. Most Buddhist monks and nuns live, study, and work in **pagodas.** Fancy carvings, painted wood, and statues of Buddha (the religion's founder) make pagodas and Buddhist temples beautiful.

Another belief system, called Confucianism, teaches people to respect and to obey their parents, teachers, and government leaders.

Some Vietnamese are Taoists. They try to live in harmony with nature. And Vietnamese Taoists believe in lots of gods and spirits, such as the Jade Emperor, who rules heaven. Many Vietnamese people combine Buddhist, Confucian, and Taoist beliefs.

Europeans brought Christianity to Vietnam, and these days some Vietnamese people are Protestant or Roman Catholic Christians. Other Vietnamese people follow both Christian and Buddhist teachings.

Vietnamese people have a lot of respect for their ancestors. Many houses have small altars covered with photos and other symbols of loved ones who have died. At certain times of year, the Vietnamese leave out food and drink for their ancestors' ghosts.

An altar (right) **dedicated to family members and respected leaders contains small gifts and family pictures.**

People perform many kinds of rituals during Tet to ensure good luck for the new year (above). Folks prepare banh chung (right)—a tasty treat for Tet!

Happy New Year!

It's Tet Nguyen Dan (New Year's Day), the most important Vietnamese holiday. Tet Nguyen Dan marks a new year and the beginning of spring. And the Vietnamese also count themselves a year older on Tet instead of on their birthday. Tet is the start of the year according to the lunar (moon-based) calendar, so the holiday falls near the end of January.

The night before Tet Nguyen Dan, families share a special meal. Fried watermelon seeds, *banh chung*, and pickled vegetables are holiday treats. Banh chung is a squishy rice cake filled with bean paste and pork, wrapped in banana leaves. At

Everyone turns a year older on Tet.

midnight, families set off firecrackers to welcome the new year.

Why is Tet so important? The Vietnamese believe that every Tet Nguyen Dan, a household god travels to heaven to report on each person's behavior during the past year. The ruler of heaven listens and then lets everyone start fresh in the new year. So folks settle fights, wear new clothes and use their best manners to get the year off to a great start. People head to the streets for parades, dances, games, and songs.

Two young Vietnamese boys eye red fireworks prepared for the Tet festivities.

The Moon Festival

The Moon Festival celebrates the autumn harvest. Boys and girls craft rice-paper lanterns in the shape of fish or stars and hang them on long bamboo poles. A candle goes inside the lantern. After dark kids carry the lit lanterns in a parade. Children munch a delicious treat called a moon cake, which is made with rice, eggs, peanuts, raisins, and watermelon seeds.

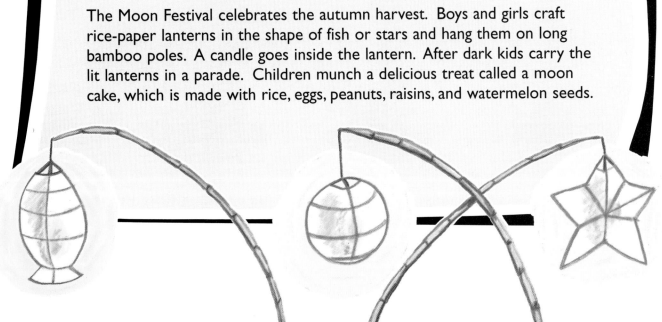

A musician plays a single-stringed zither. The lacquerware instrument is beautifully carved and decorated.

Sing It **Loud**

Most music in Vietnam is played during religious rituals and for the theater. Vietnamese musicians bang drums, gongs, and cymbals. Wind instruments, such as the bamboo flute and the Chinese oboe, are part of Vietnamese orchestras. String instruments are important, too. A dried gourd, a curved stick, and a long copper wire make an instrument called a *dan bau*.

Young people in Vietnam enjoy *quan ho*. Here's how it works. During spring festivals, boys sing a verse of a song that they make up on the spot! Girls reply with a different melody and words. But during the rest of the year, young folks tend to listen to pop music.

Music is played on many occasions, including during religious ceremonies (left).

Workers who labor in the rice paddies or who cast fishing nets sing at their tasks. Boating songs, fishing songs, and lyrics about famous rulers, brave warriors, and heroic deeds make days pass quickly. That's right—the Vietnamese love music! Some of the tunes are hundreds of years old.

These folks bang out some tunes on the stone xylophone, called a *to rung*. Different sized stones are chosen for the sounds they make when struck.

35

Talk to **Me**

Vietnamese is the official language of Vietnam. Traditional Vietnamese comes from a mix of languages spoken by the first groups of settlers in Vietnam, especially the Chinese. Vietnamese has a lot in common with Chinese, but some words and pronunciations are different in each language.

Speaking Vietnamese is like singing a song. There are high tones and low tones, changing tones and flat tones. A word can have one of many different meanings, depending on the tone a speaker uses. If you say the word *ma* in a high tone, you mean "mother." In a low tone, it means "rice plant." And with a flat tone, the word means "ghost!" If you're not careful you might say to a Vietnamese friend, "Is that your ghost?" instead of, "Is that your mother?"

**Characters decorate
a Hanoi doorway.**

Hundreds of years ago, folks used **characters** (symbols) to write Vietnamese. But these days people write Vietnamese with the same alphabet used to write English. In most words, each **syllable** is written separately, so the Vietnamese write *Vietnam* as "Viet Nam." Small lines or other symbols above or next to the letters indicate their tone. The Vietnamese call this form of writing *quoc ngu*. It is the modern official writing system used, but the old system of using characters is preferred for fancy signs and important documents.

While characters are still used for decoration (top), **Vietnamese is more commonly written in quoc ngu** (right).

Read Me **a Poem**

Poetry is BIG in Vietnam. Not only is it very popular, but poems can be hundreds of verses long! In fact, *Kim Van Kieu*—Vietnam's national poem—has 3,250 verses! Authored more than 200 years ago, the poem tells of the hardships faced by a young woman named Thuy Kieu. Because the Vietnamese language has a musical sound, listening to poetry can be really fun!

Folktales, myths, and legends are important to the Vietnamese, too. Puppet theaters and stage actors dramatize them for audiences. And, of course, the tales are great to read out loud.

Vietnam's most famous folktale is the *Legend of 100 Sons*. It's the story of a mountain spirit named Au Co, who married Lac Long, a dragon from the ocean. The couple had 100 sons who hatched from 100 eggs. Lac Long wanted to return to the sea, but Au Co wanted to live in the mountains. Half of the children stayed in the mountains with their mother. The other 50 went to the seacoast with their father. According to the legend, the sons who went to the sea became the Vietnamese people.

A True Story?

There was actually a long-ago king named Lac (who wasn't a dragon!). He ruled the early Vietnamese people of the Red River Valley, where lots of traditional Vietnamese culture developed. The Vietnamese love the *Legend of 100 Sons*. In fact, a special festival honors Lac Long every year! Older people dress in fancy silk robes, and young women carry flowers and fruit in a parade. Everyone watches fireworks and listens to traditional Vietnamese tunes.

Game **Time**

In Vietnam most people work or study hard all day long. So they like to make the most of their time off. In the cities, kids head to ice-cream parlors. Young adults often go to nightclubs or discos, where they can dance to pop music. Older people choose dance halls, where they listen to Vietnamese singers.

In the countryside, people like to visit one another's homes. They might play cards, chat, or tell stories to pass the time. Many towns have

A group of women perform martial arts in a park in Ho Chi Minh City. Morning exercises are an everyday ritual for many Vietnamese.

community centers with pool tables or televisions. Some grown-ups spend their free time taking classes, where they might learn a foreign language or a trade.

To keep fit and to have fun, many Vietnamese youngsters play soccer, volleyball, or tennis. Some Vietnamese take up **martial arts,** such as tai chi chuan. Before school, students meet at a park for tai chi chuan and for other exercises. On hot days, kids cool off with a dip in a river or in the South China Sea.

Exploring the shores of the South China Sea (above) **is a great way to pass the time on a hot day.**

The pool table at this community center (right) **is a popular hangout spot.**

Water-puppet musicians move across the surface of the black water, acting out traditional Vietnamese folktales.

Water **Puppets**

On holidays Vietnamese kids love to watch puppet shows—especially *nuoc roi* (water puppetry). A pond is the stage!

Grown-ups and kids sit on the shore of a pond or stream. Puppeteers stand up to their knees in water, hidden behind a bamboo screen. One puppeteer sets off a single firecracker, letting the audience know that the show's about to begin.

Using underwater rods, the puppeteers make the brightly painted wooden puppets glide over the water. A clown marionette tells the story that the other puppets act out. Short versions of legends and folktales are popular performances.

A nighttime favorite is shadow puppetry. Puppet-makers trim tough leather into the shapes of royalty, animals, magical creatures, and heroes. The audience sits in front of

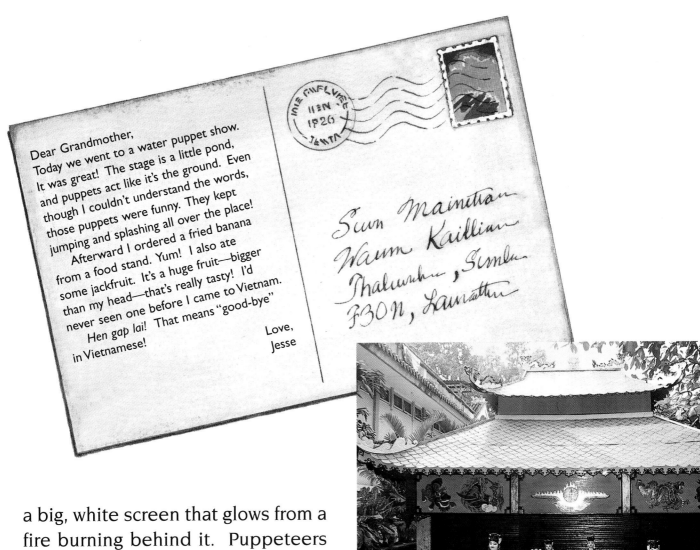

Dear Grandmother,
Today we went to a water puppet show.
It was great! The stage is a little pond,
and puppets act like it's the ground. Even
though I couldn't understand the words,
those puppets were funny. They kept
jumping and splashing all over the place!
Afterward I ordered a fried banana
from a food stand. Yum! I also ate
some jackfruit. It's a huge fruit—bigger
than my head—that's really tasty! I'd
never seen one before I came to Vietnam.
Hen gap lai! That means "good-bye"
in Vietnamese!

Love,
Jesse

a big, white screen that glows from a fire burning behind it. Puppeteers stand to the sides of the screen and make the puppets dance and jump. The audience can see the puppets' shadows on the screen. Musicians play traditional tunes, and a narrator tells a story or reads a familiar poem.

A beautifully decorated building hides the puppeteer from the audience. The puppets seem to move like magic.

Vendors sell branches of cherry and apricot flowers in the weeks before Tet. The Vietnamese believe the blossoms will bring good luck for the coming year.

Glossary

ancestor: A long-ago relative, such as a great-great-great grandparent.

character: A graphic symbol used to represent a word or letter.

Communism: A system of government in which the state (rather than private individuals) owns and controls all or most farms, factories, and businesses.

delta: An area where a river branches into many channels before reaching its mouth.

ethnic group: A large community of people that shares a number of social features in common such as language, religion, or customs.

ethnic Vietnamese: People who are descended from ancient Chinese settlers in the Red River Valley and who make up the largest ethnic group in Vietnam.

French Indochina: Modern-day Laos, Vietnam, and Cambodia when under French rule from the 1880s until 1954.

Indochina: A peninsula in Southeast Asia on which lies Laos, Cambodia, Vietnam, Thailand, Myanmar, and West Malaysia.

mangrove: A tropical tree that grows in wet areas.

martial arts: Several types of combat and self-defense, such as tai chi chuan and karate, that are practiced both as an art form and as a sport.

monsoon: A wind that blows rain to southeastern parts of Asia, such as Vietnam.

pagoda: A part of a Buddhist temple.

peninsula: A piece of land that has water on three of its sides. The fourth side is connected to land.

plain: A broad, flat area of land that has few trees or other outstanding natural features.

rain forest: A dense, green forest that receives large amounts of rain every year. These forests grow in places with a tropical climate.

silkworm: A kind of moth. The caterpillar spins a cocoon that is used in making the fabric silk.

syllable: A unit of spoken language that represents sound groupings within a word.

tropical: A region or climate that is frost-free with temperatures high enough to support year-round plant growth.

Slippery as an Eel

Boys and girls in some rural areas love an eel-catching contest that's part of Tet Nguyen Dan. The kids sing and dance in pairs, while they try to catch an eel in a jar of water. The first pair to catch the slippery creature wins.

Pronunciation Guide*

ao dai	OW YIE
Au Co	OW KAH
banh chung	BAHN CHIHNG
chanh	CHAHN
chao mung den Vietnam	CHOW MUHNG DEHN vee-EHT-nahm
cyclo	SY-cloh
dan bau	YAHNG BOW
hen gap lai	hehn GOHP ly
Ho Chi Minh	HOH CHEE MIHN
Kim Van Kieu	KIHM YUHN KAY-oh
Lac Long	LOHK LAHNG
My Nuong	MY ⁿOHNG
non la	NAHN LAH
nuoc cham	NOOK CHAHM
nuoc roi	NOOK ROY
pho	FOH
quan ho	KWAHN OH
quoc ngu	KWAHK NOO-oo
Tet Nguyen Dan	TEHT ⁿWEEN DAHN
to rung	TOH RUHN
Vietnam	vee-EHT-nahm

*Pronunciations are approximate.

46

Further Reading

Brittan, Dolly. *The People of Vietnam*. New York: Rosen Publishing Group, 1997.

Cole, Wendy. *Places and People of the World: Vietnam*. New York: Chelsea House, 1989.

Dien, Tran Van and Winabelle Gritter. *Folk Tales for Children*. Chicago: National Textbook Company, 1996.

Dooley, Nora. *Everybody Cooks Rice*. Minneapolis: Carolrhoda Books, Inc., 1991.

Gibbons, Alan. *The Jaws of the Dragon*. Minneapolis: Lerner Publications Company, 1994.

Jacobsen, Karen. *Vietnam*. Chicago: Children's Press, 1992.

Kalman, Bobbie. *Vietnam: The People*. New York: Crabtree Publishing Co., 1996.

Lorbiecki, Marybeth. *Children of Vietnam*. Minneapolis: Carolrhoda Books, Inc., 1997.

Nguyen, Chi and Judy Monroe. *Cooking the Vietnamese Way*. Minneapolis: Lerner Publications Company, 1985.

Schmidt, Jeremy and Ted Wood. *Two Lands, One Heart*. New York: Walker & Co., 1995.

Scoones, Simon. *A Family from Vietnam*. Milwaukee: Steck-Vaughn, 1998.

Shalant, Phyllis. *Look What We've Brought You from Vietnam*. New York: Julian Messner, 1988.

Vietnam in Pictures. Minneapolis: Lerner Publications Company, 1998.

Wright, David K. *Enchantment of the World: Vietnam*. Chicago: Children's Press, 1989.

Metric Conversion Chart

WHEN YOU KNOW:	MULTIPLY BY:	TO FIND:
teaspoon	5.0	milliliters
Tablespoon	15.0	milliliters
cup	0.24	liters
inches	2.54	centimeters
feet	0.3048	meters
miles	1.609	kilometers
square miles	2.59	square kilometers
degrees Fahrenheit	5/9 (after subtracting 32)	degrees Celsius

Index